CLAUDE LORRAIN
& MODERN ART

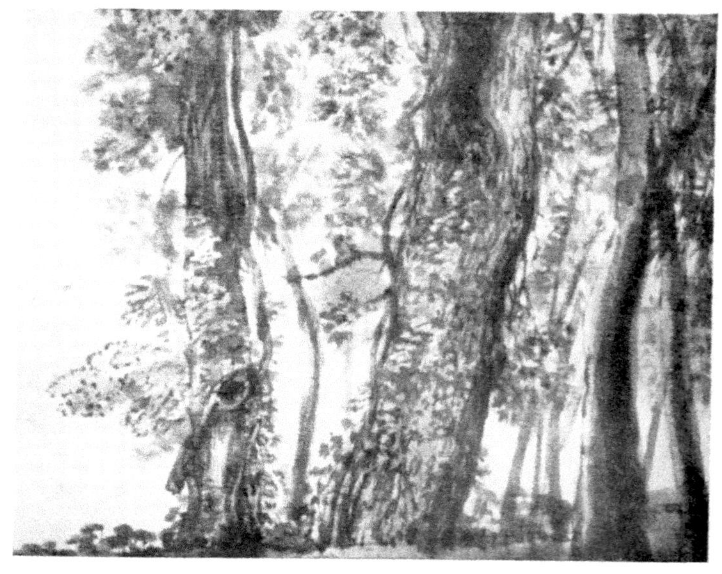

TREE TRUNKS AND FOLIAGE *Bistre drawing by Claude Lorrain*

CLAUDE LORRAIN & MODERN ART

THE REDE LECTURE
MCMXXVI

by

A. M. HIND

CAMBRIDGE
AT THE UNIVERSITY PRESS
MCMXXVI

CAMBRIDGE
UNIVERSITY PRESS

University Printing House, Cambridge CB2 8BS, United Kingdom

Cambridge University Press is part of the University of Cambridge.

It furthers the University's mission by disseminating knowledge in the pursuit of education, learning and research at the highest international levels of excellence.

www.cambridge.org
Information on this title: www.cambridge.org/9781107505704

First published 1926
First paperback edition 2015

A catalogue record for this publication is available from the British Library

ISBN 978-1-107-50570-4 Paperback

LIST OF DRAWINGS REPRODUCED

CLAUDE LORRAIN & MODERN ART

THE last century has been a period of astonishing progress in science and the mechanical arts, and the measure of material progress has been reflected in kaleidoscopic changes in the modes of artistic expression. Modern life is too complex and its pace too great to allow of the smooth running stream of tradition; the old practice of apprenticeship has disappeared, and mass education in the schools has taken its place. The most regrettable factor is an exaggerated individualism, which emphasises the small differences and forgets or even derides the large tracts of agreement between new and old. In fact in spite of the superficially startling novelty of much modern art, continued reflection inclines one to ask whether there *is* such a thing as progress in the arts, and whether the so-called new things are not for the most part newly emphasised old things: flux and reflux with here and there a new mode or manifestation.

Contemporary criticism tends to exaggerate the relative values of fresh manifestations, forgetting the experiments of the past, and often failing to recognise certain elements of expression until they are over-emphasised. This kind of criticism is the worst temptation to young painters, inclining them to attach undue importance to subsidiary things. Thus cubism is an excellent aid, but entirely unsatisfying as an end in itself; many old masters must have used it in the studio, and here and there a relic of their study may be noted, such as the sixteenth century drawing by Luca Cambiaso, a *Scene in a Hall of Justice*, which I recently saw at a London dealer's, and illustrate in a slide.

As another example of the nearness of old and new I would instance Tintoretto's picture of *Christ walking on the Waves* in the collection of Arthur and Alice Sachs, New

York, recently published in *Apollo* by Professor Borenius; and a fine seascape by Pieter Brueghel the elder, at Vienna, shows equally astonishing analogies with modern work in its reduction of detail to suggestive shapes almost geometrically conceived.

One never hears the last of the three-dimensional character of certain phases of modern art, commonly traced back to Cézanne. But in this relation there has been no real progress since the full Renaissance, only the great painters of the fifteenth and sixteenth centuries had too much to say to fall victims to a mere fetish. A drawing of *Kalkreuth* by Albrecht Dürer, at Bremen, one of his early body-colour landscapes, probably done before the end of the fifteenth century, shows as much solidity and depth as anything of Cézanne, and is surprising in its anticipations of recent artists such as Marchand.

In fact, taking a limited period of one art,

i.e. painting and drawing from the time of the Renaissance to the present day, it is noteworthy how few are the essential changes, and the really novel elements. And going back centuries more in history, increasing knowledge of such fields as Chinese and Egyptian art only increases one's conviction that in art as in literature new manifestations and modes (such as the novel in literature and the easel picture in art) depend rather on local and temporary conditions than on higher or lower developments of genius.

Certain characteristics of great paintings are essentially individual and of their time, *e.g.* the mannerisms of Botticelli's work, and it may be generally assumed that the repetition of such characteristics is mere artificiality and not renewed life, the reason why so much Praeraphaelite work has not secured the permanent place that contemporary critics expected. And even in their original manifestations, qualities which can with any justice be called mannerisms are perhaps secondary in value to other elements of style which repeat themselves naturally at different periods in the hands of the great masters. It is possibly on this account that we can find nothing more modern than the draughtsmanship of Michelangelo, Rembrandt and Claude.

Not that these more universal elements of style are devoid of manner, for the expression of nature in art must always find its conventions entirely dissociated from photographic resemblance. Nevertheless, I think it will be found to be true that the most universally accepted conventions in draughtsmanship are those which suggest nature with as much truth as is compatible with the character of the medium used. This will certainly hold good in regard to the pen drawings of trees and foliage by Rembrandt, Claude and Turner; and in the very highest sense in regard to those by Rembrandt.

It is a salutary practice for painters and

critics who wish to preserve their modesty and balance to look back from time to time on these comparative elements, whether in the sounder and more universal conventions, or in the more experimental modes that characterise certain periods but recur in isolated instances in others. And I have chosen Claude as my *point de départ*, because to most people during the last half-century he has become the representative of a dead tradition and a bad exponent of it at the best.

I believe Ruskin to be one of the greatest writers on art (perhaps the greatest of all), for in spite of his perversities of judgment (which are often the impassioned outpourings of a moment), his works are full of an illumination that pierces to the heart of things; and modern critics and painters would do better to search for the things they say, said better, amid the judgments they regard as false, rather than deride him for those judgments without opening his books.

Read this before going to see an exhibition of modern French drawings (written in reference to the painting of water, *Modern Painters*, Vol. I, Part II, Sect. v, Chap. i, but it might equally refer to any part of nature): "Constant and eager watchfulness and portfolios filled with actual statements of water-effect, drawn on the spot and on the instant, are worth more to the painter than the most extended optical knowledge. Without these all his knowledge will end in a pedantic falsehood; with these it does not matter how gross or how daring here and there may be his violations of this or that law; his very transgressions will be admirable"... and he then proceeds to praise the effect of an oblique horizon line used by Rubens. He might even have approved an impossible table by Duncan Grant or Vanessa Bell!

And in face of his usual dogmatism and his manifest inability (traditional and physical) to realise certain great elements in art, read this disarming admission after a scathing criticism of Van de Velde and Bakhuysen (*Modern Painters*, Vol. I, Part II, Sect. V, Chap. i): "I may be wrong or they may be wrong, or at least I can conceive of no principle or opinion common between us, which either can address or understand in the other; and yet I am wrong in this want of conception, for I know that Turner once liked Van de Velde...and Turner could not have liked Van de Velde without *some* legitimate cause."

With these introductory remarks to explain something of my veneration of Ruskin, I have less hesitation in attacking those of his judgments which have been largely responsible for blinding the English public to the great qualities of Claude Lorrain. And it must always be remembered that they were the judgments of a genius scarcely past his undergraduate stage.

Here is one passage in question (*Modern Painters*, Vol. I, Part II, Sect. I, Chap. vii):

"Claude had, if it had been cultivated, a fine feeling for beauty of form, and is seldom ungraceful in his foliage; but his picture, when examined with reference to essential truth, is one mass of error from beginning to end"; and another (*Modern Painters*, Vol. I, Part II, Sect. VI, Chap. i): "It is curious that in Salvator's sketches or etchings there is less that is wrong than in his paintings; there seems a fresher remembrance of nature about them. Not so with Claude. It is only by looking over his sketches in the British Museum, that a complete and just idea is to be formed of his capacities of error; for the feeling and arrangement of many of them are of an advanced age, so that we can scarcely set them down for what they resemble, the work of a boy ten years old; and the drawing, being seen without any aids of tone or colour to set it off, shows in its naked falsehood."

And then you all know the definition of an 'Ideal' landscape in his preface to the 2nd edition of the first volume of *Modern Painters*, *i.e.* "A group of the artist's studies from nature, individually spoiled, selected with such opposition of character as may insure their neutralizing each other's effect, and united with sufficient unnaturalness and violence of association to insure their producing a general sensation of the impossible"—applying it in detail and with the most biting satire to the famous picture of *The Mill* in the National Gallery:

"The foreground is a piece of very lovely and perfect forest scenery, with a dance of peasants by a brook-side; quite enough subject to form, in the hands of a master, an impressive and complete picture. On the other side of the brook, however, we have a piece of pastoral life; a man with some bulls and goats tumbling headforemost into the water, owing to some sudden paralytic affection of all their legs. Even this group is one too many; the shepherd had no business to drive his flock so near the dancers, and the dancers will certainly frighten the cattle. But when we look farther into the picture, our feelings receive a sudden and violent shock, by the unexpected appearance, amidst things pastoral and musical, of the military; a number of Roman soldiers riding in on hobby-horses, with a leader on foot, apparently encouraging them to make an immediate and decisive charge on the musicians. Beyond the soldiers is a circular temple, in exceedingly bad repair; and close beside it, built against its very walls, a neat watermill in full work. By the mill flows a large river with a weir all across it. The weir has not been made for the mill (for that receives its water from the hills by a trough carried over the temple), but it is particularly ugly and monotonous in its line of fall, and the water below forms a dead-looking pond, on which some people are fishing in punts. The banks of this river resemble in contour the later geological formations around London, constituted chiefly of broken pots and oyster-shells. At an inconvenient distance from the water-side stands a city, composed of twenty-five round towers and a pyramid. Beyond the city is a handsome bridge; beyond the bridge, part of the Campagna, with fragments of aqueducts; beyond the Campagna, the chain of the Alps; on the left, the cascades of Tivoli."

But what, you will ask, is all this to do with modern art? Is not this classic art of Claude the very antithesis of modern ideals in landscape?

In the first place I would say that I am using the word modern in a wide sense, and will embrace in my argument examples of work from the beginning of the nineteenth century, with an occasional earlier reference. In the second, though Richard Wilson and Joseph Vernet, and in a looser sense Turner and Corot, are the more direct successors of the classic Claude, yet here and there in quite recent art one finds a reaction towards the classic, in artists such as Philip Padwick, and Algernon Newton (*e.g.* a little landscape by the latter exhibited in the Spring Exhibition of the New English Art Club of this year), and with the revival of interest in the Baroque there is every likelihood of this revival spreading to landscape.

Admitting the superiority of the Doria Palace version of *The Mill* over the National Gallery replica (which Claude did a year later), particularly in its wonderful passages of distance, sunlit plain and hill, nevertheless there are present in the replica all those great qualities in the drawing and massing of trees emulated by Turner in so many of his compositions, of which *Crossing the Brook* in the National Gallery is a superb example. Thanks to Turner himself the National Gallery offers perfect opportunity for comparing the paintings of the two masters. The juxtaposition of Turner's *Dido building Carthage* with

Claude's *Embarkation of the Queen of Sheba* may rightly lead us to regard Turner as a master of greater breadth and virtuosity in all the elements of his craft, in the detailed knowledge of the truths of natural form as well as in command of the figure. There is some unfairness perhaps to Claude that the comparison should be focussed on a somewhat stilted seaport, which, with all its advantage in purity of colour over Turner's work, hardly stands against the subtly gradated variety of treatment exhibited by Turner. But in general it is only here and there that a large landscape composition by Claude can be found in which the whole picture bears out the several virtues of its detail, or its colour. We know from his contemporary biographer, Joachim Sandrart, that Claude worked in the studio with extraordinary care and elaboration, only achieving by constant re-paintings and glazings those subtle harmonies of tone and colour within a limited scale (generally of blues and greys) which characterise his later pictures. An example lent to the Ashmolean Museum by Mrs W. F. R. Weldon, *Ascanius and the Stag*, exhibits those qualities to perfection, but it also shows the limitations of his art in a certain frigidity of treatment which seems to betray the artist disciplining himself to a conventional mode that was not entirely in his own temper.

When Poussin painted a landscape there is no doubt that the classic convention perfectly responded to his genius. He was a more purely intellectual painter than Claude; a born thinker and composer, who would make fewer mistakes than Claude in the studio because of a greater intellectual grasp and memory, not for any intimate knowledge or love of nature. Claude, on the other hand, was first and foremost a supreme lover of nature, a craftsman rather than a thinker, yet a craftsman who could rise by his very intuitions to an intensity of mood and feeling, which even Turner never achieved. In his early years he was out whole days in the Campagna contemplating nature, particularly at sunrise and sunset, and is known to have made a practice of painting in oil as well as drawing from nature. Many of his earlier pictures of the smaller size were possibly begun out of doors in this way, and only completed in the studio, and few of his so-called capital pieces touch the beauty of some of these less ambitious canvases. I would instance the little *Woodland Landscape with the Rest on the Flight into Egypt* in the collection of Sir Herbert Cook at Richmond as one of the most lovely of its kind.

Claude's genius would to my mind have blossomed more fully in the nineteenth century; for he was a naturalist at heart, driven by the classical conventions of his period rather than by his own bent into his more elaborate classical compositions. His drawings from nature show him, for the most part, less constrained and more truly himself than his pictures, and in these he touches common ground with many modern landscape painters, and rises to an achievement, which can only be rivalled in its own field by Rembrandt and Turner. It is regrettable that he seldom allowed himself to develop the simpler schemes of his drawings into completed pictures. But the achievement of this freedom in painting remained for the nineteenth century.

Coming to certain more specific comparisons of Claude's work with modern art, and limiting our survey to his drawings, I hope to refer you to enough material to form a "complete and just idea of Claude's capacities of error" and the way in which modern artists have continued the same perverse traditions. Even Ruskin allowed Claude the glory among painters of having set the sun in the heavens, and there is no question that in the treatment of diffused sunshine Claude was the great forerunner of the nineteenth century. Not that he was in any sense isolated in this relation, for he had worthy, though secondary, followers in artists like Jan Both, and there were several other Dutchmen of the seventeenth century, notably Aelbert Cuyp and Jacob Ruysdael, who mastered an even greater variety in the expression of sun, storm and cloud.

Sunlight in trees has seldom been more beautifully painted than in Sir Herbert Cook's *Rest on the Flight*, and a drawing of a *Sunlit Wood* in the Teyler Museum (reproduced on the opposite page), and another of *Tree Trunks and Foliage* in the same collection, which I illustrate in the Frontispiece, show how in the pen and bistre wash in which he executed most of his drawings, Claude obtained effects which seem even more magical because of the simplicity of the medium.

I would ask you with this example and

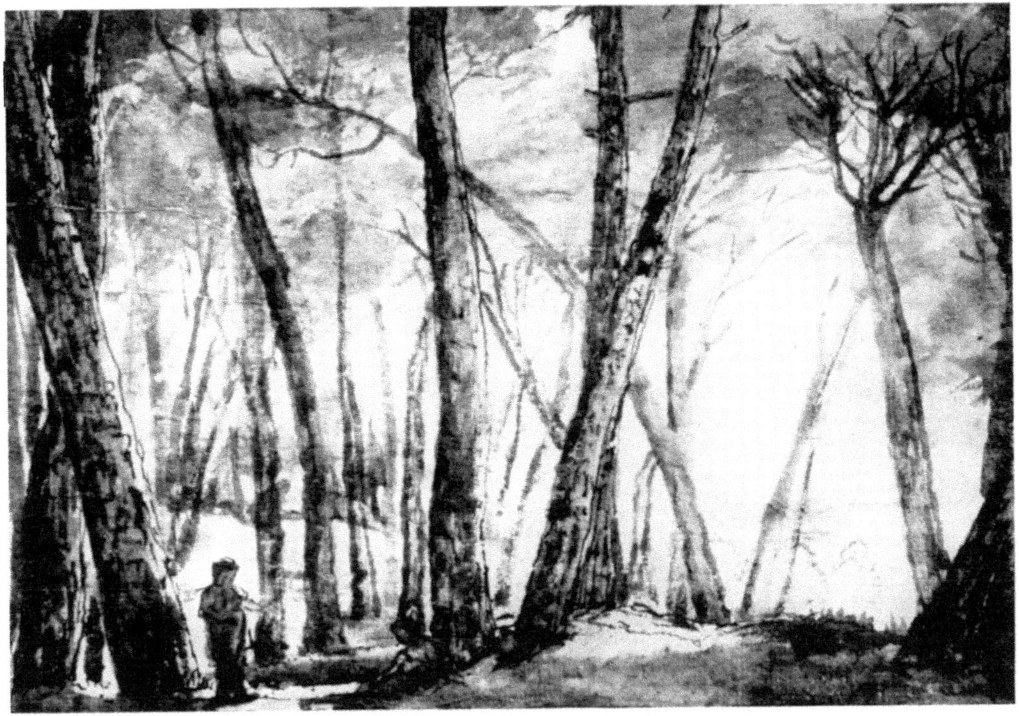

SUNLIT WOOD

Bistre drawing by Claude Lorrain

others that follow before you to compare the qualities of Claude and Turner as draughtsmen in this medium of pen and wash. The drawings by Turner that one inevitably cites are those he did as studies for the engravings of his *Liber Studiorum*, in which he was admittedly inspired by emulation of Claude's *Liber Veritatis* (the series of Claude's own records of his compositions, now preserved at Chatsworth), which had been engraved by Richard Earlom and published in 1777. Most of the studies for this series are now in the Tate Gallery, which also possesses a certain number of similar drawings probably done for the same purpose but never engraved.

First the *Procris and Cephalus* (*Liber Studiorum*, 41) as a fairly near analogy of sunlit wood, though here we have the last evening rays instead of the warm misty sunlight of Claude's wood. The one point of comparison that I would make in this case is between the simplicity of Claude's method in which the pen and wash does its work unaided except by the tone of the paper; while in Turner the rendering of gleams of light is helped out by abrasion of the surface of the paper. There is convincing truth in Turner's conventions in the drawing of trees and foliage, but not more than is shown by Claude in his more explicit drawings such as the magnificent *Oak and Ivy, Villa Madama, Rome*, to cite one among many in the British Museum.

Turner's more complex method, and his dependence on abrasion for his high lights is shown again in his study for the *Bridge in the Middle Distance* (*Liber Studiorum*, 13), a drawing of extraordinary virtuosity. But here, though superficially like Claude, Turner is working on an entirely different basis; and rather as a painter than a draughtsman, for the subtle rendering of gradations of light in cloud and sky is done by the most delicate paintings and re-paintings. It is unreasonable to dogmatise on what should or should not be a proper use of watercolour; for it is generally a matter of individual feeling, and varying capabilities and ends of expression. But one may nevertheless express a personal preference for the draughtsman or water-colourist who imposes limitations on his methods, which may restrict his field of expression, but certainly fortify what remains. And Claude, like Rembrandt, kept for the most part to the purest use of wash, with as little re-washing as is compatible with a due variety of tone and values. As an example of Claude's simplicity of expression of land, water and cloud, I refer you to a drawing of a *Seaport with Stormy Sky* in the collection of the Earl of Leicester, and add another comparison to show Claude's relation to the century that preceded him in a landscape drawing at Darmstadt which has been recently attributed to Titian by Baron von Hadeln. Personally I am more inclined to think that the so-called Titian may be a Claude, but whichever it is, we at least have an indication in this example of one of the main sources of Claude's landscape.

I would next oppose another of Turner's *Liber Studiorum* studies, the *Bridge and Goats* (43), to Claude for another reason, *i.e.* the comparison of their respective qualities in the use of line. Here Turner's drawing is chiefly in pen, with only a light wash, and no abrasion of the paper, so that the character of the line is easy to estimate. Comparing the treatment of distance with the same in such a drawing as Claude's little *View in the Campagna*, from the Malcolm collection in the British Museum (141), I have little hesitation in regarding Turner's line as almost pedestrian in face of Claude's magic. And another quality of Claude's art that comes out in this little sketch is his instinct for simple massing in composition, which is as manifest in his treatment of the receding plains of an extensive landscape, as in his superb grouping of trees.

It brings to one's mind in recent British art the peculiar virtue of D. Y. Cameron's work, and in spite of difference of medium his painting of *Ben Ledi* in the Tate Gallery (to take one example) is not far removed in spirit. There is something again of the same mood in each. Perhaps this is an element outside the mere pictorial quality, more appertaining to the poetic sense, and depending in Claude and in Cameron more on their oneness at heart with their respective landscapes, with the Roman Campagna and the Scottish Mountain and Moorland.

In poetic mood Alphonse Legros is of the same kin, and apart from many etchings to which one might refer, he left numerous drawings in Claude's medium of pen and bistre wash which are haunted by the spirit of the earlier master.

That this poetic sense in landscape painting

or drawing is compatible with simple and truthful rendering of natural scenery, lovers of English watercolour would never dispute. The situation is analogous to that of Wordsworth in poetry. But with Claude's paintings chiefly in mind, it is less commonly realised how natural and ungarnished Claude could be in his drawings, and how often the simplest of these reveals the essential poetry of his nature. Some years ago Mr R. R. Tatlock published in the *Burlington Magazine* (XXXVIII, 4) a drawing of the *Lago di Bracciano*, in the collection of Professor Borenius, against a recent photograph of the lake from nearly the same point of view, and the comparison proved convincingly how little invention was used in this instance.

Claude's kinship in his more naturalistic drawings with French landscape art of the eighteen 'thirties is most clearly shown in the *Full River after Rain* of Christ Church Library, Oxford, if one could be quite certain of the attribution, which is only recent. The old mount bears an eighteenth-century ascription to Rembrandt (manifestly in error), but held against the light figures are revealed, drawn in red chalk on the covered back of the sheet, which hardly look like Claude. If there should be any chance of removing the backing without damage to the drawing, more light may be thrown on the problem. And in the *Willows skirting a Country Road* of the British Museum (49), one might again imagine oneself in the early nineteenth century, and this time rather in England than in France. It reminds one also of Van Dyck, whom you probably seldom think of for his landscape drawings, and a study to which I would refer you, a body-colour *View of a Country Lane* in the British Museum (87), shows a similar subject to the Claude, in which the English flavour is probably based on an actual English lane, and offers a more definite example of the parentage of English watercolour.

Nor are some of the more modern phases of French and English landscape drawing without their counterpart (I will not say inspiration) in Claude. A *Woodland Glade* in the British Museum (37) is one of several examples in which the artist shows the same joy in the harmonious, and sometimes quaint, rhythms of curving tree trunks, as one sees in an artist such as Paul Nash.

Finally I would speak of Claude's relation to modern art in the remarkable freedom of his use of watercolour wash and in what might loosely be called impressionism. Not impressionism in the technical sense in which it has been applied to the nineteenth-century movement (which aimed at reflecting in colour one side of natural truth), but impressionism in its more literal interpretation as the expression either of passing aspects of nature, or of more permanent aspects, by summary and suggestive means. The *Impression of a Woodland Road with High Banks*

(British Museum, 54) is a striking example, in which the merest suggestion of detailed form is combined with a most forcible treatment of light and shade, and composed in a rhythm which anticipates Gainsborough.

Nocturne, in the same collection (55), is equally summary in its drawing, and in its subtle rendering of light has sometimes been compared with Whistler. Perhaps this is little more than in the name, and its truer modern affinities are with the more vigorously impressionistic drawings of Sargent, Brabazon and Steer. But in some ways it is more suggestive of a Watteau-like scene in a villa garden, in which artificial illumination is contrasted with the moonlight affected by Claude's Dutch contemporary, Aart van der Neer.

My earlier comparisons with Turner drawings have not been entirely in favour of Turner, but the two further examples in the

Tate Gallery, of which I shall speak, show him as great a wizard as Claude in the use of bistre wash. They are both drawings which were probably done for the *Liber* though never engraved, but brushed with a freedom which anticipates his later work in a full watercolour palette. The *Trees by a Lake* (CXVIII, g.) is in the purest wash, a most beautiful and suggestive impression of evening light; the *Study of Lake and Mountains* (CXV, 48) is equally subtle, but its magical effect is helped out by wiping out lights by various means in the wash before it dries into the paper, a method in which C. A. Hunt is particularly skilful among present-day watercolour painters. A wonderful drawing by Rembrandt, in the Bonnat collection, of *Trees reflected in Water* (H. de G. 763) is remarkable in its affinities to Claude and Turner, in fact so nearly allied to Turner that one might have been tempted, if there had not been actual writing in Rembrandt's hand on the reverse of the sheet, to think it by Turner himself.

Another of the most lovely of twilight studies comparable with Claude is the *Trees at Evening* by Alexander Cozens, now lent to the Tate Gallery by Mr Edward Marsh. There is a gentleness of mood and expression in this example which is more characteristic of Claude than Cozens, who in his method of blot-drawing sometimes carried boldness of wash to extremes in which strength was rather superficial than inherent.

My comparisons and remarks have shown you English watercolour art as the chief modern reflection of Claude's qualities as a draughtsman. And before I close I would deprecate the tendency of some recent critics to detract from the virtue of watercolour in general. Of course it is an art that has always tempted young ladies to inefficient and pretty effects, yet this should not be allowed to derogate from the noble work done in the medium, whether in monochrome or colour, by such masters as Claude, Rembrandt, and Turner. If further argument were needed, one might turn to William Blake, or to Oriental art, but Turner's latest watercolours are enough to show that the material slightness of a medium bears no relation to greatness of achievement.

I end with two specimens of Claude's drawing which I would have you compare with recent English watercolours, and notably with Wilson Steer. The *Study of Rocks and Trees with a Church Tower in the Distance*, in the Teyler Museum, Haarlem, is a very typical example of Claude's superb strength of light and shade, a direct study from nature entirely free from any attempt at enhancement of effect by scheme of composition, and in that respect, as well as in its freedom of wash, thoroughly modern. As a study also it may be noted how it keeps near solid earth by its partial drawing in detail of some of the foliage.

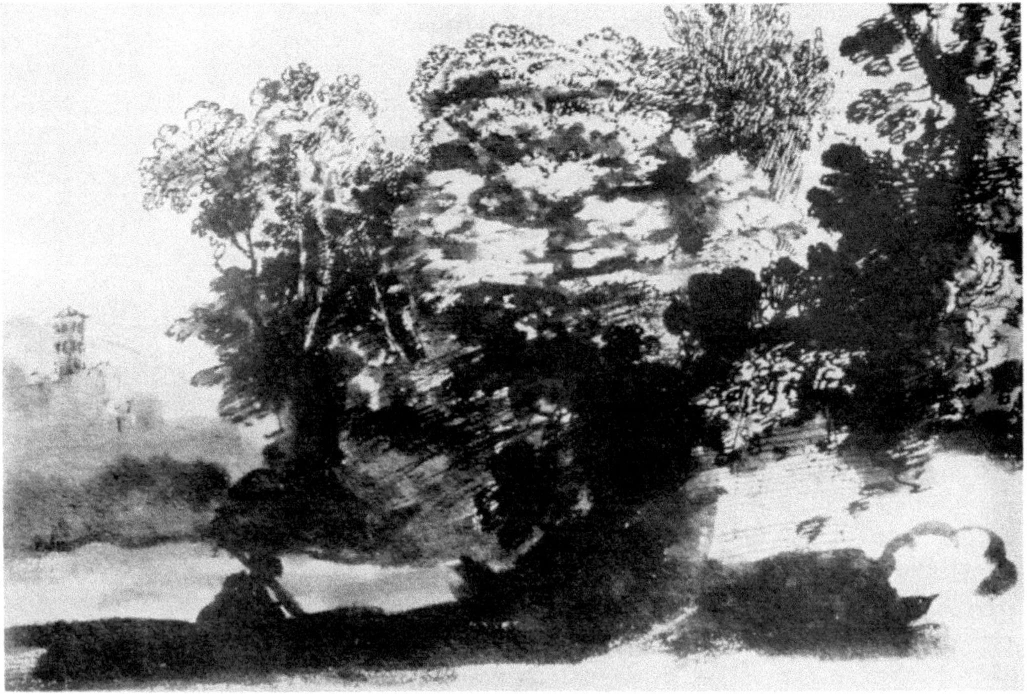

STUDY OF ROCKS AND TREES *Bistre drawing by Claude Lorrain*

The study of *Elm Trees* by Wilson Steer (1924), recently presented to the Tate Gallery by Mr A. E. Anderson, is without even this partial drawing of detail; Ruskin would certainly have called it 'Blottesque' and condemned it, and in this sense it is the true descendant of Alexander Cozens and John Constable; but its bold suggestion leaves me with the impression of a complete structural command, with no suggestion of the "disorderly, slovenly and licentious" methods of which Ruskin held Cox and Constable guilty.

'Blottesque,' too, is my last example of Claude, the *Tiber above Rome*, in the British Museum (27), and an incomparable achievement in the same "licentious" vein.

Steer has pursued the method with a consistently increasing sacrifice of other elements of drawing besides wash; but as long as the true understanding and sense of structure are inherent in the impression (and real knowledge is required to discern the true from the false), the aim is entirely legitimate in itself and justified by its works. It is not a safe method to recommend to the young painter's exclusive devotion, and Ruskin is a sound teacher in declaring that "the brush is at once the artist's greatest aid and enemy; it enables him to make his power available, but at the same time it undermines his power, and unless it be constantly rejected for the pencil, never can be rightly used" (*Modern Painters*, Vol. I, Part II, Sect. III, Chap. iv).

Claude never limited himself in his modes of expression in drawing (except in keeping largely to the one medium of pen and bistre); he was always adapting his manner to the subject in hand, always sensitive to the response of nature in her various manifestations and moods, and on this account, if on no other, his achievements in methods which have been more exclusively practised by modern draughtsmen are invariably fresh and convincing.

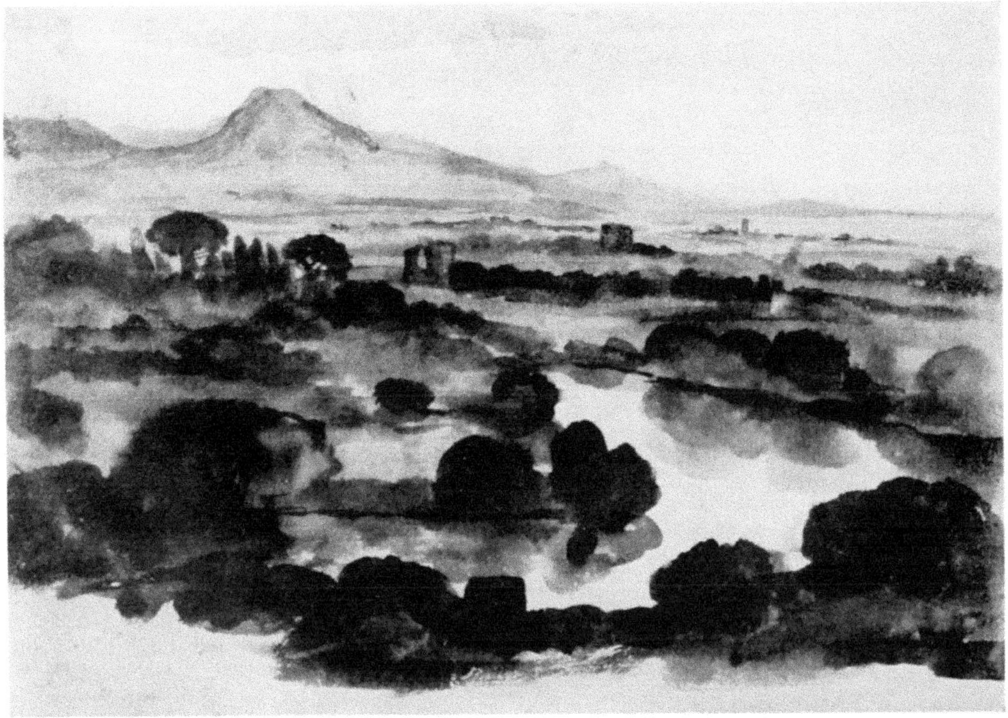

THE TIBER ABOVE ROME

Bistre drawing by Claude Lorrain

For EU product safety concerns, contact us at Calle de José Abascal, 56–1°, 28003 Madrid, Spain or eugpsr@cambridge.org.

www.ingramcontent.com/pod-product-compliance
Ingram Content Group UK Ltd.
Pitfield, Milton Keynes, MK11 3LW, UK
UKHW020223250726
13967UKWH00001B/162

* 9 7 8 1 1 0 7 5 0 5 7 0 4 *